ABC San Antonio

An Alphabet Guidebook to the Fiesta City

To Dave

ABC San Antonio

An Alphabet Guidebook to the Fiesta City

By Heila Rogers

Photographs by
David Rogers
Haley Beham
Heila Rogers
Christopher Borchardt
and Daniel Rogers

Stage Books
San Antonio, Texas

FIRST EDITION

Library of Congress Control Number: 2009911513
Library of Congress-in-Publication data is available upon request.

Printed and bound in San Antonio, Texas by Litho Press.

ISBN No. 978-0-9824695-0-7
ABC San Antonio, An Alphabet Guidebook to the Fiesta City

Publisher's Note: Neither Stage Books, LLC nor the author has any interest, financial or personal, in the locations listed in this book. While every effort was made to ensure that all data was accurate at the time of publication, we advise verifying to confirm details.

On front cover: SeaWorld San Antonio, The River Walk photos by David Rogers
On back cover: Skyline photo by Haley Beham, Traffic Sign photo by Christopher Borchardt
Asian Festival Dancer, The Institute of Texan Cultures - www.texancultures.com,
Longhorns photos by Haley Beham
On the dedication page: Fiesta Ribbons photo by Heila Rogers
On the previous page: Pooch Parade photo by David Rogers
On this page: Open Sign photo by Haley Beham
On page 33: Portrait of the author and G. Nuño by Haley Beham

Can you find these letters around San Antonio?

Locations on the following page

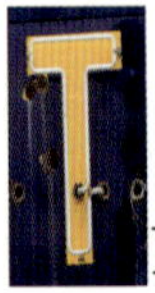

This project was a pleasure and an adventure to complete. As I criss-crossed San Antonio driving and on foot, it was a pleasure to meet people and have them share favorite parts of the city, funny memories, or stories about the area. I'm thankful for every kind word and moment of shared laughter.

After the example of G. Augustine Lynas whose own book *The ABCs of Central Park* helped to inspire this one, I have avoided "baby words" in the text of this book. When I asked a local children's librarian what she thought about "X" being for xerophyte she said that she thought it should work if the child were reading along with someone, in a learning context. So "X" is for xerophyte! Yes, I had to look it up, too. (See the guidebook section.) HR

I hope you enjoy this representative montage of letters from all over town.

Here are the addresses you'll need for your own Alphabet Scavenger Hunt. Have fun touring the city! HR

A - The Alamodome, 100 Montana St. #101
Photo by Dave Rogers

B - Bill Miller restaurants, locations throughout the city. Photo by Dave Rogers

C - Carver Community Cultural Center, 226 N. Hackberry. Photo by Dave Rogers

D - The Dominion Country Club, 1 Dominion Dr.
Photo by Heila Rogers

E - H-E-B grocery store, 1520 Austin Hwy
Photo by Dave Rogers

F - Garden for the Blind, San Antonio Botanical Garden, 555 Funston @ N. New Braunfels Ave.
Photo by Christopher Borchardt

G - "Chinese" Tea Garden sign, at the Japanese Tea Garden, 3875 N. St. Mary's St.
Photo by Daniel Rogers

H - Temple Beth-El, 211 Belknap Pl.
Photo by Dave Rogers

I - Basilica of the National Shrine of the Little Flower, 824 Kentucky Ave.
Photo by Dave Rogers

J - The University of Texas Health Science Center at San Antonio, 7703 Floyd Curl Dr.
Photo by Heila Rogers

K - Sunken Garden Theater, 3875 N. St. Mary's St.
Photo by Daniel Rogers

L - Ranch Motel, 3101 Broadway St.
Photo by Daniel Rogers

M - Menger Hotel, 204 Alamo Plaza
Photo by Dave Rogers

N - Olmos Basin Park, Jones Maltsberger Rd. & Basse Rd. Photo by Heila Rogers

O - Tower of the Americas, 600 HemisFair Park
Photo by Dave Rogers

P - The Lion & Rose, 5148 Broadway
Photo by Daniel Rogers

Q - Augies Barbwire Smokehouse, 3709 N. St. Mary's St.
Photo by Daniel Rogers

R - Olmos Pharmacy, 3902 McCullough Ave.
Photo by Daniel Rogers

S - Fort Sam Houston, E. Grayson & N. New Braunfels gate
Photo by Heila Rogers

T - Casa Dos Laredos, 1701 Guadalupe St.
Photo by Dave Rogers

U - Teresita's, 901 N. New Braunfels
Photo by Heila Rogers

V - Mission San Juan Capistrano, 9109 Graf Rd.
Photo by Dave Rogers

W - Landa Library interior steps, 233 Bushnell
Photo by Abigail Rogers

X - Texas specialty license plate
Photo by Dave Rogers

Y - "Trinity" mural, 1105 S. Trinity St.
Photo by Dave Rogers

Z - San Antonio Zoo, 903 N. St. Mary's St.
Photo by Dave Rogers

Aa

is for Arts Night at The Alamo
and antiques in a row.

Bb is for baby, benches and big boots.

Cc is for cowboys, crowds and cottages.

Dd is for dancers and ducks.

Ee

is for eating egg tacos for breakfast.

Ff

is for fountains
and a float for Fiesta.

Gg

is for growing, green gardens, with guests.

Hh is for historical house and horses.

Ii is for instruments and instructions.

Jj is for jump.

Kk is for kolaches and kings.

Ll

is for libraries and longhorns.

Mm

is for mission, mosaic and mural.

Nn is for neighbors.

Oo

is for an
open sign
and a very
large oak
overhead.

Pp is for party store and prize-winning piñata.

Qq is for queen's dressmaker and quarry.

Rr

is for ride on a river.

Ss is for sculptures and skeletons.

Tt

is for two types of trains.

Uu is for universities.

Vv is for a variety of valiant volunteers.

Ww is for whales in water and wreath.

Xx is for xerophytes.

Yy is for yelling and yellow rose of Texas.

Zz is for zoo and Zanco.

Meet Ten San Antonians

A lot of the motivation for this section came from a desire to honor Mary Lou Artz and the essential behind-the-scenes work she has been doing in San Antonio for decades. Her graciousness and ability caused me to want to feature her in some way. So hers is the first interview in "Meet Ten San Antonians." The rest follow in the order in which we met. There is no rank system to be implied, simply a tool to help children become familiar with the basic numerals. I hope you enjoy their company as much as I did. Another big thank you to all, for your openness and generosity and your contributions to our community.

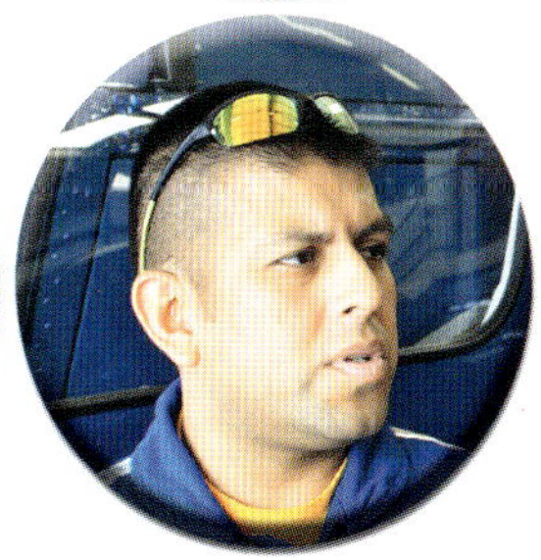

1

Mary Lou Artz, Cowgirl Couturier

Jars of rhinestones, paper templates of intricate designs and yards of specially selected grand fabrics are transformed by hand into magnificent long trains and beaded dresses. Mary Lou has been working since 1975 for the Fiesta San Antonio tradition of the Coronation of the Order of the Alamo. Her husband Ted has helped make wire-framed headpieces and custom-built tables for the studio. Along with her teams of assistant dressmakers and other studios across town, they create fabulous outfits worn by twenty-six women each year. Eight months of the year they gradually complete 7 or 8 dresses with trains. San Antonians as well as tourists from all over the world come to see the results of their painstaking craft each April. Posed photos of past creations and their wearers line the walls of Mary Lou's workroom, stunning in their variety and beauty, and in the concept of the amount of work they represent. The gorgeous, beautiful handiwork of these dedicated dressmakers is impressive and fairytale-like.

HALEY BEHAM

Mary Lou Artz in her studio/workroom.

2

Becky Meyers, Cake Baker

Birthdays, weddings and holidays have something at their center. That something happens to be Becky's job. When she was thirteen, she designed and baked a fancy, three-tiered cake for her birthday. She and her friends dressed up in lacy dresses, hats and pearls for the party. Young Becky didn't know at the time that becoming a Pastry Chef was in her future. She attended culinary school and learned about everything from the chemical properties of ingredients to how to specifically combine them. She gathered favorite recipes along the way from books, online and school. Her love for cakes continues. A friendly business owner lets her use the industrial-size oven she needs for baking. Then she covers a round confection with an initial "crumb coat" of frosting and sets it on a spinning stand. The final coat of buttercream is decorated with swirls, ribbons or rows of tiny dots. Her creations taste as good as they look. Whether carrot or chocolate, the term "melt in your mouth" applies.

HALEY BEHAM

Becky Meyers at work in her kitchen.

3

James Garcia, Improv Teacher

James' teaching is a lot like musical improvisation. An improv musician feels their way into a completely new, created-on-the-fly piece, while connecting it to what has been played before, and the context of the place, performance and people involved. This is what James does with each guitar student. He tries to establish and meet them at a point where they can connect over the instrument and the playing of it. James was given his own first guitar at age nine, but it wasn't until he was eleven that he taught himself how to tune the guitar and finally liked the sound. He began to play chords, was hooked and has practically never been without a guitar since. Playing for hours on end growing up he practiced or strummed sometimes even while reading a book. One of James' favorite places in San Antonio is La Tuna on Saturday nights for the live music. The crowd is a mixture of people and a relaxed vibe. Kind of like his approach to life.

HEILA ROGERS

James Garcia at Alamo Music Center.

4 Mark Outing, Host of Substance

Most folks wouldn't have seen potential in the boarded-up building Mark passed one day dropping his kids at school, but he felt a strong urge to stop and find out about the property. He remembered, "With God all things are possible." A few minutes later when he checked with the owner she handed him the keys on the spot. The bright yellow-and-black Fatty's restaurant is now a favorite for burgers near the downtown area. Shadows of birds in flight against a sky blue background are painted across the side of an old refrigeration company warehouse opposite the restaurant. When I met Joshua, Mark and his wife Joyce's four year old son, it wasn't two minutes of "small talk" before he said, "Whyn't you come over for some burgers?" At that point I didn't even know who his daddy was, but his sincerity and emphasis were convincing. Mark says his favorite part about the restaurant is interacting with the people he serves.

DAVID ROGERS

Mark & Joyce Outing at Fatty's Burgers & More.

5

Barney Smith, Museum Creator

Barney Smith's former professional life as a master plumber prepared him to work with his current artistic medium. Years of owning a Texas ranch, hunting, and traveling also provided plenty of material for his themes. Mr. Smith created his first piece years ago when searching for a suitable mount for a pair of deer antlers. He found the perfect size and weight object in a toilet seat lid, and hasn't turned back since. Themes of over 850 seats so far, include keys, candy dispensers, arrowheads and Texas. There is one lid with a piece of the Space Shuttle "Challenger," one with a piece of "Saddam's toilet," and a few for geocaching and letterboxing enthusiasts. Barney's double-wide, metal garage where the collection is housed is stuffed to the gills with boxes of items he might need, has saved, or wants to use for future creations. Mr. Smith has become somewhat of a minor national celebrity, but it's the force of his personality, his stories and his charisma that make him a pleasure to visit.

HEILA ROGERS

Barney Smith at his Toilet Seat Art Museum.

6

Gabriel Nuño, Zapatero

To enter his shop is to enter another world. One where leather reigns, the pungent smell of glue pervades, and pride of heritage is evident. A place where the bell over the door tinkles frequently. Gabriel's skills and experience are much in evidence when he's at work behind the repair counter of the store. His movements have the assurance one sees in professional athletes. He's not dribbling or shooting a ball, but dipping and stroking a brushful of glue or scraping a heel with a stiff brush. When he was fourteen in Mexico, he sat around a low table day by day for a year with his father and his father's friends. He was watching them, listening and practicing. He has run his own business here in San Antonio now for more than 35 years. The machines Mr. Nuño uses are old-fashioned but functional, as shown by the fresh black heel dust covering them. One heavy, oversized sewing machine has a special thin arm that a shoe fits over in order to be patched. Steadiness and honesty seem as evident in this place as the stacks of foot-shaped pads piled everywhere for replacing worn-out soles.

HEILA ROGERS

Gabriel Nuño & his son Miguel at Southside Boot & Shoe Repair.

7

Ausencio Mata III, Safety Flier

Ausencio keeps people safe from high above the city. As a police helicopter pilot he chases suspects from the sky. Special night-vision equipment lets him and his colleagues track fleeing offenders after dark. Working together as a team with officers on the ground, suspects can be captured before they cause harm. "Aussie's" facial expressions are calm but alert. He can just as easily glide into a smile as into intense concentration. He and the other Blue Eagle pilots fly with a co-pilot at all times and with radio ear pieces. They take turns piloting the chopper. The co-pilot does the tracking, and keeps a close lookout for aircraft safety issues like power lines and trees. Making joint decisions quickly is essential. Ausencio says that one thing he appreciates about San Antonio is how grateful many of its citizens are to their law enforcement personnel. He also enjoys fishing at Lake Calaveras.

DAVID ROGERS

Ausencio Mata at SAPD Helicopter Unit headquarters.

8 Irene Canaria, Hair Sculptor

Irene started her career braiding her dolls' hair. Enamored with the new skill, she began "braiding excessively" on anyone who would let her get hold of her. She remembers unplugging other more mundane electrical appliances like clocks in order to plug in curling irons. After obtaining a degree in music she realized she had interest and abilities in another creative field and completed training as a stylist. When I suggested that a good haircut is similar to a good sculpture, she talked about cutting techniques and how she can use those to apply to different types of hair and people. She can picture in her mind a finished style to create. This ability being similar to the way she can picture the "shape" of a piece of music and then play it. Also like an ensemble group of musicians, she likes working as a team with other stylists and beauty consultants. Irene loves dancing, and one of her favorite places in San Antonio is Sam's Burger Joint on Swing Nite.

HALEY BEHAM

Irene Canaria at K. Charles & Co. preparing an "Infinity" style for a Hair Fashion Show.

9 Kathleen Trenchard, Paper Puncher

Kathleen strikes hard on a sharp metal chisel with a heavy rubber hammer. A lead pad underneath the tissue paper she's cutting, is put there to absorb the blows. And there are a lot of blows. Each tiny space between the connecting pieces of the main design needs to be cut out for light or color to come through and be part of the final image. Kathleen remembers the first time she saw a delicate, lavender papel picado in a San Antonio art gallery. Papel picado means "punched paper" in Spanish. The piece was lit from behind and hung so that any air currents moved it gently. It fascinated and delighted her so much that right then her artistic medium of specialty was born. Researching the method of Mexican papercutting even led her to write a book, and she's created different products, from baby shower invitations to public art pieces, using this folk-art form. A permanent exhibition of her work at the AT&T Center mezzanine consists of giant, intricately cut plastic panels. Kathleen enjoys bicycling around the historic King William district.

HALEY BEHAM

Kathleen Trenchard at work in her studio.

10

Heila Rogers, Wordsmith

Heila (pronounced "Hyla") enjoys making things with words. Playing with and shaping them to try and find just the right meanings and combination. She gets fascinated and sidetracked trying to remember a specific word when speaking and will say things like "What's that one that starts with a 'c' and means happy?" Because Heila enjoys reading a lot she therefore doesn't know how to pronounce many words because she's only seen them in print. For example, "detritus." She enjoys meeting people and getting into conversations about their mutual experiences of life. Heila has liked children's books since her own childhood. Two of her favorite authors are Beverly Cleary and Ralph Moody. She has always wanted to be Agatha Christie's Miss Marple for Halloween. Every time she moves to a new city with her family, she likes to explore the unique things there are to see and do. Then she can't wait to tell others about them, preferably in writing. Her favorite place in San Antonio, without question, is the beautiful Landa Library.

DANIEL ROGERS

Heila Rogers at work in her home office.

INDEX

I've included in this guidebook section not only a list of San Antonio sights and their locations, but interesting anecdotal information and useful websites. The information corresponds to the photos on the letter pages.

a

The Alamo - www.thealamo.org

Luminaria - "Arts Night in San Antonio"
www.luminariasa.org

There are several antique shops on Hildebrand between Breeden & Beacon. Photos by Haley Beham

B

Faux bois sculptures throughout town by the Cortes family - Bench at La Cantera shopping center
www.studiocortes.com - Photo by Dave Rogers

Mosaic bench at Guadalupe Cultural Arts Center - www.guadalupeculturalarts.org - Photo by Heila Rogers

North Park Mall - world's largest cowboy boots
Photo by Haley Beham

C

Cowboy entertaining the crowd for the San Antonio Stock Show & Rodeo opening ceremony. You'll see big belt buckles and fancy chaps as well as gigantic animals and amazing athletes. www.sarodeo.com - Photo by Haley Beham

The cottage district in Alamo Heights - Around April's Fiesta, people string their homes and businesses with flags (papel picado). The vibrant colors and cut-out patterns create a party-like atmosphere. Photo by Heila Rogers

D

Dancers at the Arneson River Theater
www.lavillita.com/arne - Photo by Haley Beham

Folks feeding water fowl at Woodlawn Lake Park
Photo by David Rogers

E

Father and son enjoy a breakfast taco at Carmelitas restaurant on Broadway. Photo by David Rogers

F

Fiesta is a ten-day celebration of city-wide activities each year, including the historic, three-hour Battle of Flowers Parade. www.battleofflowers.org - Photo by David Rogers

Extensive water gardens have multiple fountains and a

nice playground near Hemisfair Plaza, which was built at the base of the Tower of the Americas, as a part of the World's Fair of 1968. Photo by Haley Beham

The Japanese Tea Garden has a large koi pond.
www.sanantonio.gov/sapar/japaneseteagardenopen
Photo by Heila Rogers

Visitor to the San Antonio Botanical Garden snaps a shot of a resident. www.sabot.org Photo by Christopher Borchardt

King William Historic District - www.kingwilliamassociation.org Photo by Heila Rogers

Charreada or Mexican Rodeo, has special clothing including sombreros and wide bowties and special events like the "pass of death" which involves a man standing on the ground doing tricks with a lasso and a running horse passing dangerously close by. - www.sacharro.com
Photos by David Rogers

Symphony member helps a young violinist at the San Antonio Symphony "instrument petting zoo" in the Spring.
www.sasymphony.org

Texas A&M "Aggies" Marching Band
Photos by David Rogers

J

McAllister Park dog park has plenty of pet play equipment.
Photo by Daniel Rogers

Blossom Athletic Park Photo by David Rogers

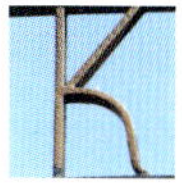

El Rey Feo - a Fiesta "King" Photo by David Rogers

Kolaches (kuh-lah-chees) are sweet breads with different fillings - an Eastern European pastry. Vegetable kolache in picture from Joseph's Storehouse Restaurant & Bakery. Raspberry & sausage kolaches from Broadway Daily Bread Co. Photo by Heila Rogers

Pooch Parade - a Fiesta event Photo by David Rogers

San Antonio Public Library Landa branch book sculpture
Photo by Daniel Rogers

The dramatic Central Library building. www.mysapl.org
Photo by Christopher Borchardt

A cattle run on Houston Street (see Index letter C) opens the anuual rodeo events in San Antonio in February
Photo by Haley Beham

You'll find hundreds of distinctive murals on the Westside of San Antonio. Check out www.sahearts.com for excellent

neighborhood information from the City of San Antonio Office of Cultural Affairs.

Mosaic at the River Walk Street Car Station
Photos by David Rogers

Mission Espada attracts numerous colorful events
Photo by Christopher Borchardt

Fiesta Pooch Parade on Arbutus St. sponsored by the Delta Society of San Antonio - www.deltasa.org

Terrell Hills Fourth of July neighborhood parade
Photos by David Rogers

Open sign at Lasting Impressions Antiques on W. Hildebrand Ave. Photo by Haley Beham

Live Oak Tree in the Alamo courtyard
Photo by Christopher Borchardt.

Elaborate, custom-made pinatas go above and beyond classic designs.

Brackenridge Park is wonderful. Many beautiful trees, walking paths, a river with fishing, and picnic tables. www.saparks.com

Amol's party supply store - Photo by Heila Rogers

Fiesta "royalty" each year includes a "queen". Thank you to the Mortimer family, owners of the 2007 train pictured whose design was influenced by the gardens of the Ottoman Empire. www.fiesta-sa.org. Photo by Haley Beham

Several places around San Antonio are built within the leftover spaces of former stone quarries, including Six Flags Fiesta Texas, a shopping center and a golf course.
Photo by David Rogers

The riverwalk winds for miles past shops, restaurants, and quiet residential areas - www.visitsanantonio.com/visitors/play/explore-the-river-walk

The "torch of friendship" was a gift to the city from the Association of Mexican Entrepreneurs of San Antonio.
Photo by David Rogers

The McNay Art Museum - www.mcnayart.org - Kinetic sculpture by George Rickey

The Witte Museum has scientific & natural history exhibits. The monument to trail drivers sculpture (detail) is by Gutzon Borglum who carved Mount Rushmore.
www.wittemuseum.org - Photos by David Rogers

A “duchess” good-naturedly “shows her shoes” in response to traditional requests from the crowd at the Battle of Flowers parade.

Young rider meets the conductors of the mini-train in Brackenridge Park - Photos by David Rogers

Our Lady of the Lake University
Photo by Heila Rogers

The University of Texas at San Antonio, Downtown Campus   Photo by Christopher Borchardt

Weekly basic training graduation ceremonies take place at Lackland Air Force Base.

Newly graduated airman salutes. Photos by David Rogers

Shamu at SeaWorld San Antonio   Photo by David Rogers

Fiesta wreaths, with flowers and ribbons, are all over town in April.   Photo by Christopher Borchardt

This xerophyte, decorated for Christmas, adapts to dry conditions by holding water in its stems and leaves. San Antonio Cactus and Xerophyte Society - www.sacxs.org
Photo by Daniel Rogers

Star Squad members instantly pose for us at a Silver Stars WNBA game, of July weekend.
Photo by David Rogers

Yellow rose in bloom at the entrance to the Sunken Garden Theater
Photo by Heila Rogers

Fish enthrall young visitors at the San Antonio Zoo and Aquarium - www.sazoo-aq.org

People dressed in re-enactment costumes at the Alamo for Luminaria (see Index letter A). Charles Zanco, one of the defenders of the Alamo, originally from Denmark, might have designed the first “Lone Star” Texas state flag.
www.thealamo.org - Photos by Haley Beham

About the Author:

Heila Rogers has always liked children's literature and earned a BA in Elementary Education from the University of Northern Colorado with a focus in Language Arts, and a certificate in Creative Writing from the University of East Anglia in the UK. She and her husband Dave, an Air Force doctor, both grew up in Greeley, Colorado. They next lived for seven years in the Washington, D.C. area where their children Abigail and Daniel were born. Since then the family has lived in Omaha, Nebraska; Mildenhall, East Anglia; Goldsboro, North Carolina and now San Antonio. There have been aspects to treasure and appreciate about each place.

Heila is grateful for the fruitful collaborative effort which became *ABC San Antonio*. To attempt to encapsulate a city of millions into 26 letters of the alphabet was an invigorating creative endeavor. It was satisfying in the end to chronicle the interaction, as we made the acquaintance of this special city and its friendly inhabitants.

To contact the author or for ordering information please go to: www.abcsanantonio.net

About the Art Director / Designer:

G. Augustine Lynas is a freelance artist / author who has lived and worked in New York City since 1965. Although he is an experienced graphic designer, his first love is sculpture. He gained world wide recognition as a sand sculptor with the publication of his book *Sandsong* and the release of his documentary film of the same name. Mr. Lynas paints murals, designs games, and writes and illustrates books (including *The ABCs of Central Park*). He has created concrete, bronze and ceramic sculptures in six NYC parks and various private collections. His work can be seen at www.SandSong.com and at www.LynasPress.com

---

Many thanks to Bekah Stolhandske for her enthusiastic, unwavering support for this project and for her editorial help. My wonderful children and husband were crucial to completion in various important ways. To friends who provided encouragement along the way, it wouldn't have happened without you. Lynas, you brought along not only experience, talent and motivation, but the heart of a teacher. Thank you.

In the beginning the Word already existed. The Word was with God, and the Word was God. He existed in the beginning with God. God created everything through him, and nothing was created except through him. The Word gave life to everything that was created, and his life brought light to everyone. John 1:1-4 NLT